My Asian
Kitchen

Linda Le

NEW HOLLAND

First published in 2015 by New Holland Publishers Pty Ltd
London • Sydney • Auckland

The Chandlery Unit 009 50 Westminster Bridge Road London SE1 7QY United Kingdom
1/66 Gibbes Street Chatswood NSW 2067 Australia
5/39 Woodside Ave Northcote, Auckland 0627 New Zealand

www.newhollandpublishers.com

A record of this book is held at the British Library and the National Library of Australia.

ISBN 9781742577012

Managing Director: Fiona Schultz
Project Editor: Holly Willsher
Cover Designer: Andrew Quinlan
Internal Designer: Peter Guo
Production Director: Olga Dementiev
Printer: Toppan Leefung Printing Limited

10 9 8 7 6 5 4 3 2 1

Keep up with New Holland Publishers on Facebook
www.facebook.com/NewHollandPublishers

Content

Daily food
IN CHINA

Three Meals For All

Most people in China work, sometimes at several jobs, since the lifting of the restraints under the Cultural Revolution, the rise of private enterprise and the increase in free markets and westernisation. Breakfast is a fast meal, likely to be milk (inevitably tinned or powdered) and either toast or a traditional baked cake with sweet or salty stuffing. Ginseng is a medicinal tea often used to greet the morning with steamed or fried bread. If there's time, congee or rice porridge will be eaten with pickles and, possibly, steamed bread or twisted fried dough-sticks with wok-cooked beancurd. Beancurd and milk with steamed dumplings is another breakfast alternative. Poor people in the countryside commonly begin with just rice and tea.

Working women and their partners are likely to opt for street stall snacks en route to work, as they do not have the time to cook as their mothers did. Breakfast might be stuffed wontons or dumplings in soup and, during the day, jasmine or green tea in the north and green tea in the south will be drunk. The Appetiser and snacks section includes recipes for some of these snacks.

Traditionally, the oldest, most able woman in a household begins to prepare the evening meal in the afternoon, to be cooked when the working family comes home. An childless couple living on their own will typically cook their own meal, based around the fan – rice, noodles, steamed bread or pancakes – with one tsai (meat or fish) dish and up to two vegetables, plus soup. Young couples are also likely to eat out on cheap snacks or restaurant food.

Festival Feast Fare

The most major festival in China is the Chinese New Year festival, which is celebrated in January or February according to the Chinese lunar calendar. There is a three-day lantern festival 15 days into the New Year. Other festivals include May Day and the two-day celebration of National Day in September or October. Some families and/or communities celebrate the birthday of Guan Yin, the goddess of mercy, on the 19th day of the second lunar month, when people bring food, often vegetarian, to her shrines. The 23rd day of the third lunar month is the birthday of Mazu, goddess of the sea and mother of heaven. Every fishing village and junk has respective temples and shrines to her. Fish-eating coastal communities eat meat on that day out of respect for her. Qing Ming, meaning 'pure and clean', is a special time devoted to honouring ancestors and dead relatives which takes place 106 days after the winter solstice festival. Graves are visited and tidied, and only cold picnic fare is eaten as no home fires are lit for two days out of respect for the dead. The year also includes the Dragon Boat, Lotus, Double Ninth and Double

Seventh festivals. The Festival of the Hungry Ghosts is held on the mainland, and in Hong Kong, as well as in Singapore and Malaysia, on the 15th day of the seventh lunar month. Burning money, clothes and offering vegetarian foods to all, appease the spirits of Buddhist Chinese who have died far from home. Mid-autumn is moon festival time when the man in the moon plays matchmaker and people exchange gifts of fruit, sweets and moon cakes.

Decorated outside with red lanterns, restaurants do brisk trade during most festivals. At birthday parties, a written character meaning longevity is placed on the wall. At a wedding, another character means double happiness. More affluent people are more commonly selecting joint-venture western hotels for marriage celebrations but, while the bride may first wear a western white gown rather than the traditional red dress, which is donned later, the menu will inevitably be Chinese.

At most meals, cold dishes, from peanuts to roasted pork, condiments and sauces await guests. To these are added hot, sweet and vegetable dishes, rice or noodles and soup. Often the dessert will arrive in the middle of the meal and, according to the customs of the region, soup may come last. In Guangzhou, even at a family dinner, eight dishes plus a soup are served. Nine courses signify everlasting friendship. In Guangdong Province, soup is served first to aid the digestive system. Sometimes desserts are served both first and last, to signify that life should be sweet from beginning to end.

The Chinese aren't very fond of desserts but fresh fruit may be served after the meal. Chinese apples are amongst the world's biggest. Chopped and tossed in toffee (see page 76), they taste delicious.

At any meal gathering, guests should leave a little food in the main dishes on the table,. The hosts will then be satisfied they have provided adequately. If the diners eat all the food, provision will be seen to be inadequate and the host will lose face.

Your Chinese Dinner Party

Imported dinner sets are inexpensive in Chinese stores and are often sold in department stores too. Each person should have a rice bowl, two smaller bowls for dipping sauces, such as soy or chilli, and a bread and butter-sized plate. Main dishes are served on large plates placed in the centre of the table, along with a large bowl of rice with a lid to keep it warm throughout the meal. Another big bowl contains soup. Two large porcelain ladles are for serving and a smaller spoon is provided for each diner to eat soup with.

In China, people often move food from the main dishes to individual plates or bowls with their own chopsticks, which is not very hygienic outside a family situation. You may like to place an extra serving spoon by each dish. Many restaurants in China set tables with a paper bag containing 'Sterilized Chopstick', meaning that the pair have not been used before nor will be used again.

When buying chopsticks, opt for plastic, wooden or camel bone pairs with the finest points, which will make picking up a single rice grain or a pea easier. To master the art of using chopsticks, rest the lower one on the fourth finger of one hand, holding it with the thumb. The third and forefinger will operate the one above, securing food between the two.

Entrees

Spring Rolls (Lumpia Goreng)

Makes about 24

Ingredients

1 tbsp peanut oil

2 cloves garlic, crushed

4 spring onions (scallions), sliced

350 g (12 oz) chicken mince

1 carrot, finely sliced

225 g (8 oz) Chinese cabbage, shredded

2 tbsp sweet soy sauce (kecap manis)

50 g (2 oz) vermicelli noodles, cooked

Spring roll wrappers

Oil, for cooking

Spring roll sauce

1 tbsp tamarind concentrate

1 tbsp soy sauce

2 tbsp water

½ tsp sambal ulek

½ tsp root ginger, grated (shredded)

½ tsp palm sugar or brown sugar

Method

Heat the peanut oil in a wok or frying pan. Add the garlic, shallots and chicken mince and stir-fry for 4–5 minutes, or until the mince is cooked. Add the carrot, cabbage and kecap manis and stir-fry for 3–4 minutes, or until cooked. Combine the noodles with the chicken and leave to cool. Place 1 tablespoon of mixture on a spring roll wrapper. Roll up and brush the ends with water.

Heat the oil in a wok or frying pan. Add the spring rolls to the work and fry for 1–2 minutes, or until golden and crisp.

Combine all the sauce ingredients in a small dish and set aside.

Drain on kitchen paper and serve with spring roll sauce.

Indonesian Beef Croquettes (Perkedel Daging)

Makes about 12 pancakes

Pancakes

150 g (5 oz) plain (all-purpose)
   flour
2 eggs, separated
475 ml (16 fl oz) water
Pinch of salt
Peanut oil, for cooking
115 g (4 oz) breadcrumbs

Filling

1 tbsp peanut oil
1 brown onion, finely chopped
2 garlic cloves, crushed
400 g (14 oz) beef mince
1–2 tsp chilli powder
1 tbsp sweet soy sauce (kecap
   manis)
225 g (8 oz) cabbage, finely
   shredded
Spring roll sauce, to serve
   (see recipe page 9)

Method

To make the pancakes, whisk together the flour, egg yolks, water and salt in a mixing bowl to make a batter.

Heat a little oil in a frying pan, just enough to coat. Tip a small amount of the batter into the frying pan to cover the surface, making them paper thin. Cook the pancakes one at a time. Cook one side only. When the batter starts to colour, remove from the frying pan. Tip onto a warmed plate to keep warm while you cook the rest of the pancakes. Cover with kitchen foil.

To make the filling, heat the oil in a frying pan. Add the onion, garlic and beef mince and fry for 4–5 minutes, or until meat is cooked through. Add the chilli powder, soy sauce and cabbage and cook for another 2–3 minutes. Leave the mixture to cool.

Meanwhile, beat the egg whites in a wide bowl. Place the breadcrumbs on a plate. Place tablespoons of filling on each pancake. Fold to form an envelope. Dip the pancakes in the beaten egg whites and then into the breadcrumbs.

Heat the oil in a wok and cook the pancakes for 1–2 minutes, or until golden and crisp. Drain on paper towel. Serve with spring roll sauce.

Crispy Seafood Wontons (Pangsit Goreng)

Makes about 30

Ingredients

100 g (3½ oz) peeled green
   prawns (shrimp)
200 g (7 oz) fish fillets, skinned
   and diced
1 garlic clove, crushed
2 green shallots, sliced
2 tsp soy sauce
1 egg
1 packet wonton skins
Peanut oil, for cooking

Wonton sauce

2 tbsp soy sauce
2 tbsp water
1 garlic clove, crushed
½ tsp root ginger, grated
   (shredded)
½ tsp palm sugar or brown sugar

Method

Combine the prawns, fish, garlic, shallots, soy sauce and egg in a food processor. Process mixture until smooth.

Place spoonfuls of mixture in the centre of each wonton skin. Brush the edges with a little water. Fold the skin in half to form a triangle and press the edges lightly to seal.

Combine the ingredients for the sauce in a small dish and set aside.

Heat the oil in a wok and cook each wonton for 1–2 minutes, or until golden and crisp. Serve with wonton sauce.

Sesame Prawn Triangles With Chilli Sauce

Serves 4

Ingredients

125 g (4½ oz) cooked peeled
  prawns (shrimp), defrosted if
  frozen
1 clove garlic, chopped
2 tbsp beaten egg
1 tsp cornflour
½ tsp sesame oil
a few drops of light soy sauce
3 slices of white bread
2 tbsp sesame seeds
peanut oil for deep-frying

Dipping sauce

1 cm (½ in) fresh root ginger,
  finely chopped
2 tbsp hot chilli sauce
juice of ½ lime

Method

Blend prawns, garlic, egg, cornflour,
oil and soy sauce to a paste in a food
processor. Alternatively, grind prawns with
a pestle and mortar, then mix with the
other ingredients.

Spread one side of each slice of bread
evenly with prawn paste, sprinkle with
sesame seeds, remove crusts and cut into
4 triangles. To make dipping sauce, mix
together ginger, chilli sauce and lime juice,
then set aside.

Heat 2½ cm (1 in) of oil in a large frying-
pan over a medium to high heat. Add half
the prawn triangles, prawn-side down,
and fry for 4–5 minutes on each side, until
deep golden. Drain on kitchen towels and
keep warm while you cook the remaining
prawn triangles. Serve with dipping sauce.

Honey And Chilli Prawns

Serves 3-4

Ingredients

500 g (1 lb 2 oz) green king
   prawns (shrimp)
soaked bamboo skewers

Marinade

60 ml (2 fl oz) red wine
175 g (6 oz) honey
¼ tsp ground chilli
1 tsp mustard powder

Method

Mix all ingredients, except prawns, together to make marinade.

Shell and devein prawns, leaving tails intact. Place in a glass dish and add enough marinade to coat well. Cover and marinate in refrigerator for 1 hour.

Thread prawns onto skewers, either through the side or through the length of each prawn.

Heat the barbecue to medium-high. Place a sheet of baking paper over the grill bars and place prawns on the paper. Cook for 4–5 minutes each side. They will turn pink when cooked. Brush with marinade while cooking. Transfer to a platter. Remove skewers and serve immediately.

Crab Meat Fritters

Serves 4

Ingredients

3 eggs

100 g (3½ oz) bean sprouts

3 spring onions (scallions),
   chopped

400 g (14 oz) crab meat

salt and cracked black pepper

oil for deep-frying

Sauce

2 tsp cornflour

1 tbsp sugar

3 tbsp soy sauce

250 ml (8 fl oz) chicken stock

2 tbsp dry sherry

Method

Beat eggs in a bowl, stir in bean sprouts, spring onions and crab meat, and add salt and pepper to taste.

Heat sufficient oil to cover the base of a frying-pan and drop in the crab mixture, one heaped tablespoon at a time.

Fry until golden brown on one side, then turn and brown the other side.

Remove from pan, and keep warm.

To make the sauce, blend together cornflour and sugar in a pan, add soy sauce and chicken stock.

Slowly bring to the boil over a low heat, stirring all the time. Cook for 3 minutes, or until sauce is thickened. Stir in sherry. Serve fritters with sauce.

Soups

Chicken and Corn Soup (Sop Ayam Jagung)

Serves 4

Ingredients

2 tsp peanut oil

1.5 litres (2½ pints) chicken stock

450 g (1 lb) shredded cooked chicken

400 g (14 oz) can sweet corn kernels, drained

2 tbsp sweet soy sauce (kecap manis)

1–2 tsp sambal ulek

225 g (8 oz) shredded English or Chinese spinach, washed and drained

Salt, to taste

Paste

2 French shallots, chopped

2 cloves garlic

2 candle nuts (or macadamias)

1 tsp terasi

2 tsp peanut oil

Method

Crush or pound the paste ingredients in a mortar with pestle or use a small food processor.

Heat the peanut oil in a large saucepan. Add the paste and fry for 1–2 minutes. Add the stock, chicken, corn, kecap manis and sambal ulek. Bring to the boil and simmer over low heat for 5–10 minutes.

Add the spinach and cook for 1–2 minutes. Season with salt. Divide between soup bowls.

Cabbage Parcels in Soup

Serves 6

Ingredients

24 cabbage leaves
6 spring onions (scallions)
20 g (¾ oz) coriander
(cilantro), finely chopped
125 g (4½ oz) tofu, crumbled
1 tbsp light soy sauce
black pepper
1.5 litre (2½ pints) vegetable
stock

Method

Blanch cabbage leaves in boiling water and cut away any tough sections from their bases.

Cut white ends from spring onions and finely chop the four white heads. Slice two for garnish. Lengthwise, halve green stalks into strips.

Mix well the chopped spring onions and half of the coriander and tofu and soy. Season with pepper.

Into each cabbage leaf, place a tablespoon of mixture and fold first the leaf base then outer edges over it and roll up. Carefully tie up each roll with a length of green spring onion then place the parcels gently into boiling stock to cook for 6 minutes.

Lift parcels into bowls, pour a 250 ml (8 fl oz) of stock over each and garnish with remaining sliced spring onions and coriander.

Fish Noodle Soup

Serves 4

Ingredients

500 g (1 lb 2 oz) white fish
fillets

vegetable oil

85 g (3 oz) spring onions
(scallions)

1 tsp chopped, fresh ginger

1 tsp garlic, chopped or crushed

1 red pepper (capsicum), seeded
and chopped

1 litre (1¼ pints) fish stock or
water

1 tbsp oyster sauce

½ tsp ground black pepper

1 tsp sesame oil

1 tbsp dry sherry

250 g (9 oz) egg noodles, boiled

1 tsp sesame oil, extra

½ red pepper (capsicum), seeded
(extra) and chopped for
garnish

Method

Chop fish into bite-sized pieces. Heat enough vegetable oil to deep-fry fish for 2½ minutes. Remove and drain. Cut spring onions into 4 cm (1½ in) sections, separating white parts from green.

Heat 3 tablespoons of oil and brown ginger and soften garlic. Add fish, pepper and white sections of spring onions. Stir-fry for 3 minutes then add stock or water and boil. Add green spring onion sections, oyster sauce, black pepper, oil and sherry and simmer for 1 minute, stirring.

Add hot, cooked, drained noodles and extra 1 teaspoon of oil. Stir through until hot. Serve immediately, garnished with chopped pepper.

Ginger Chicken WonTon Soup

Serves 6-8

Ingredients

Soup

1 tbsp sesame oil

1–2 tsp chilli paste

1 tbsp soy sauce

2 cloves garlic, minced

45 g (1½ oz) fresh ginger, sliced

1¾ litres (3½ pints) chicken
   stock

200 g (7 oz) can bamboo shoots

6 spring onions (scallions),
   sliced diagonally

Wontons

4 fresh shiitake mushrooms

1 tsp five spice powder

100 g (3½ oz) water chestnuts,
   drained

3 spring onions (scallions),
   chopped

3 sprigs coriander

2 tbsp soy sauce

1 tbsp fresh ginger, grated

1 fresh bird's-eye chilli, minced

1 tbsp sesame seeds

2 chicken breast fillets, skin off

1 pack wonton wrappers

Method

First, make the soup. Heat sesame oil in a saucepan and add chilli paste, soy sauce, garlic and ginger and sauté for 1–2 minutes. Add stock and simmer for 15 minutes then add bamboo shoots and sliced spring onions. Set aside.

Now make the wontons. Place all the ingredients, except wonton wrappers, in a food processor and 'pulse' the mixture until it is well chopped. Do not overprocess.

To shape wontons, separate wonton wrappers and lay them out on a bench. Place 1 tablespoon of filling in the centre of each wrapper. Working with one wrapper at a time, pick up wrapper and moisten the edges with water. Fold wrapper into a triangle, pinching the pastry together well to enclose the filling. Then wrap the triangle around your finger, carefully pinching together the opposite corners. Shape each wonton in this way.

Add the wontons to the simmering soup and cook them for about 4 minutes. Serve immediately.

Mains

Poultry

Javanese Curried Chicken (Ayam Jawa)

Serves 4

Ingredients

2 tbsp vegetable oil

4 chicken thighs

1 onion, chopped

3 garlic cloves, crushed

1 stick lemongrass, finely chopped

1 tsp root ginger, grated (crushed)

1 tsp ground coriander

1 tsp ground turmeric

½ tsp ground cumin

250 ml (8 fl oz) coconut milk

6 curry leaves

20 g (¼ oz) coriander (cilantro) leaves

Plain rice, to serve

Method

Heat the oil in a frying pan. Add the chicken and cook for 4–5 minutes, or until golden. Add the onion, garlic, lemongrass and ginger. Cook until the onion is soft, about 5 minutes. Add the ground coriander, turmeric and cumin and cook until aromatic.

Add the coconut milk and curry leaves and simmer uncovered for 15–20 minutes, or until the sauce has thickened. Stir through the coriander leaves. Serve with plain rice.

Roast Spiced Chicken (Ayam Panggang Pedis)

Serves 4

Ingredients

2 tbsp margarine

2 garlic cloves, crushed

2 tbsp sweet soy sauce (kecap manis)

2 tbsp tamarind concentrate

2–3 tsp sambal ulek

1.5 kg (3¼ lb) chicken, cleaned

Wedges of lime, to serve

Method

Preheat the oven to 200°C (400°F).

Heat the margarine in a small saucepan. Add the garlic and cook for 1–2 minutes. Add the kecap manis, tamarind and sambal ulek. Bring to the boil. Remove from the heat and brush over the chicken.

Place the chicken on a rack over a baking dish. Cover lightly with foil and bake for 30 minutes. Remove the foil, baste the chicken and bake for another 20–30 minutes, or until cooked.

Cut the chicken into pieces and serve with lime wedges.

Crispy Fried Duck (Bebek Goreng)

Serves 4

Ingredients

2 tbsp soy sauce

1 tbsp tamarind concentrate

1 tbsp peanut oil

1 tsp root ginger, grated (crushed)

1 garlic clove, crushed

1 tsp ground coriander

4 duck breasts

60 ml (2 fl oz) peanut oil, for cooking

Salad greens, to serve

Method

In a bowl, combine the soy sauce, tamarind, oil, ginger, garlic and coriander to make a marinade. Place the duck in a shallow non-metallic container and pour the marinade over the top. Leave to marinate in the refrigerator for 2–3 hours.

Preheat the oven to 200°C (400°F).

Heat the oil in a frying pan. Add the duck and cook for 1–2 minutes or until golden and crisp. Place the duck on a rack set over a shallow baking dish and cook for 15–18 minutes. Slice and serve with salad greens.

Stir-fried chicken with almonds and broccoli

Serves 4

Ingredients

500 g (1 lb 2 oz) chicken strips

5 tsp cornflour

½ tsp Chinese five spice powder

½ tsp salt

oil for cooking

150 g (5 oz) blanched almonds

2 cm (¾ ins) piece fresh ginger,
    finely chopped

1 clove garlic, crushed

2 tbsp dry sherry

1 tsp sugar

1 tbsp soy sauce

2 tsp water

200 g (7 oz) broccoli florets,
    blanched

boiled rice, to serve

Method

Place the chicken in a bowl and sprinkle over 3 teaspoons of the cornflour, the five spice powder and salt. Mix well and set aside. Heat oil in the wok and fry the almonds until golden. Remove, drain and set aside. Add the ginger and garlic and stir-fry for one minute. Add the chicken in batches and stir-fry until the chicken turns white.

Return all the chicken to the wok, add the sherry, sugar and soy sauce and stir a little. Combine the remaining cornflour with the water, then add to the chicken. Stir until the sauce thickens.

Add the broccoli and fried almonds and toss to heat through. Serve immediately with boiled rice.

To blanch broccoli, place in a saucepan of boiling water for 30 seconds or until it turns bright green. Remove immediately and plunge into a bowl of iced water. When cold, drain in a colander.

Chicken Rice with Pineapple (Nasi Kebuli)

Serves 4

Ingredients

2 tbsp butter or oil

500 g (1 lb 2 oz) boneless chicken, diced into 1 cm (³/₈ in) cubes

750 ml (1½ pt) chicken stock

1 tsp salt

400 g (14 oz) long-grain rice, washed and drained

½ small pineapple, peeled and sliced then cut into small pieces, to serve

Fried shallot, to serve

Seasoning

13 shallots, peeled and finely chopped

7 garlic cloves, peeled and finely chopped

2.5 cm (1 in) piece of root ginger, peeled and chopped

1 tsp coriander

½ tsp white peppercorns

½ tsp cumin

Nutmeg, freshly grated

8 cm (3 in) cinnamon stick (quill)

4 cardamom pods, bruised

2 cloves

1 lemongrass stalk, bruised

Method

Heat the butter or oil in a wok or heavy saucepan. Add all the seasoning ingredients and sauté for 2–3 minutes. Add the chicken and continue sautéing for 3 minutes over high heat.

Add the chicken stock and salt and simmer until the chicken is tender. Strain the stock and put chicken pieces aside.

Put the rice in a rice cooker or heavy stock pot, add 550 ml (18 fl oz) of the reserved chicken stock and bring to the boil. Cover the pan and simmer until the rice is almost cooked and the liquid is absorbed. Add the diced chicken and cook over low heat until the rice is thoroughly cooked.

Serve on a platter garnished with fried shallots and pineapple pieces.

Asian Chicken Curry

Serves 4

Ingredients

500 g (1 lb 2 oz) chicken thigh
    fillets

2 tbsp oil

1 large onion, finely chopped

250 ml (8 fl oz) Madras curry
    sauce

2 tbsp sultanas

2 bananas, sliced

1 green apple, peeled and cut
    into large dice

Method

Cut chicken thighs into 3 pieces. Heat half the oil in a large saucepan, add $\frac{1}{3}$ of the chicken and quickly brown on both sides. Remove to a plate and brown remaining chicken in 2 batches, adding remaining oil when necessary. Remove last batch of chicken.

Add onion and cook a little then stir in the curry sauce. Quarter-fill the can with water to rinse down remaining sauce and then pour into saucepan.

Bring to the boil, turn down heat and return the chicken to the saucepan. Cover and simmer for 20 minutes. Add sultanas, banana and apple and simmer 15–20 minutes more. Serve immediately with boiled rice.

Javanese Chicken and Vegetables (Ayam Jawa Sayur)

Serves 4

Ingredients

2 tbsp peanut oil

500 g (1 lb 2 oz) chicken thigh
    fillets

3 shallots, sliced

2 garlic cloves, crushed

2 tsp root ginger, grated
    (crushed)

1 tsp ground turmeric

1 tsp ground coriander

1 tsp ground cumin

1 tsp galangal powder

250 ml (8 fl oz) coconut milk

175 ml (6 fl oz) chicken stock

2 tsp sambal ulek

1 stalk lemongrass, bruised

2 salam leaves (use curry leaves
    or bay as an alternative)

1 carrot, sliced

2 potatoes, diced

150 g (5 oz) green (French)
    beans, sliced

Plain rice, to serve

Method

Heat the oil in a large saucepan. Add the chicken and cook for 4–5 minutes, or until golden. Add the shallots, garlic and ginger. Cook until the shallots are soft. Add the turmeric, coriander, cumin and galangal powder. Cook until aromatic.

Add the coconut milk, chicken stock, sambal ulek, lemongrass and salam leaves. Bring to the boil. Add the vegetables and cook for 10–15 minutes, or until the vegetables are tender. Serve with plain rice.

Chicken Satay
(Sate Ayam)

Makes about 12

Ingredients

12 bamboo skewers

500 g (1 lb 2 oz) chicken thigh
    fillets, diced (beef, lamb and
    pork can also be used)

2 tbsp peanut oil

2 tbsp sweet soy sauce (kecap
    manis)

1 tbsp soy sauce

1 garlic clove, crushed

Peanut sauce, to serve

Method

Soak the bamboo skewers in cold water for
15–20 minutes.

Thread diced chicken onto the bamboo
skewers. Arrange in a large, shallow dish.

Combine the peanut oil, soy sauces and
garlic in a bowl and stir to combine. Pour
the marinade over the chicken and leave to
marinate in the refrigerator for 1–2 hours.

Cook the satays on a barbecue for
10–15 minutes, or until cooked through.

Serve with peanut sauce.

Indonesian Chicken Rolls

Serves 4

Ingredients

1 kg (2 lb) chicken thigh fillets

285 g (10 oz) can rendang curry
  sauce

2 bananas

2 tbsp vegetable oil

120 ml (4 fl oz) water

120 ml (4 fl oz) coconut milk

1 small pineapple, peeled and
  thinly sliced

freshly ground black pepper

20 g (¾ oz) butter

2 tbsp shredded coconut, toasted

steamed white rice, to serve

Method

Open out the thigh fillets on a large
chopping board. Flatten with a meat mallet
to an even thickness. Spread each with a
teaspoon of rendang curry sauce.

Peel bananas and slit in half lengthwise
then cut in half to make 4 pieces. Place a
piece of banana in centre of each fillet and
form into a roll. Fasten with a toothpick.
Heat oil in a wide-based saucepan and
brown the rolls on all sides, a few at a time,
removing rolls to a plate as they brown.
Drain all the oil from the saucepan.

To the same saucepan, add remaining
curry sauce and the water. Bring to the
boil, turn down heat to a simmer and
add the chicken rolls. Cover and simmer
35 minutes, turning rolls once during
cooking.

Remove rolls to a heated platter and keep
hot. If sauce is thin, increase heat and
reduce sauce to a thicker consistency.
Reduce heat and stir in the coconut milk
and simmer 2 minutes. Return rolls to the
saucepan to reheat.

Sauté the pineapple rings in the butter
until lightly coloured and grind over some
black pepper. Arrange 1 or 2 slices of
pineapple and a chicken roll on each plate,
spoon sauce over the roll and sprinkle with
a little toasted coconut. Accompany with
steamed rice.

Teriyaki Chicken

Serves 4

Ingredients

3 tsp/15 ml sugar
60 ml (2 fl oz) sake
60 ml (2 fl oz) mirin
125 ml (4 fl oz) light soy sauce
4 chicken thighs

Teriyaki can be applied to a wide variety of meats and seafood. Teriyaki fish cutlets, prawns, beef and squid are just a few. These can be barbecued or grilled using this versatile marinade.

Method

To make marinade, combine sugar, sake, mirin and soy sauce.

Bone the chicken thighs, leaving skin intact.

Place chicken into a dish, add about half the teriyaki marinade and marinate for 6–8 hours.

Remove chicken from marinade and place on barbecue about 20 cm (8 in) from moderate coals.

Cook for about 45 minutes, or until cooked.

Add remaining marinade to a saucepan and reduce to about half. Serve with the cooked chicken.

Sweet and Sour Chicken

Serves 4

Ingredients

500 g (1 lb 2 oz) chicken thigh
   fillets
450 g (1 lb) canned pineapple
   pieces
1 red pepper (capsicum)
6 spring onions (scallions)
2 tsp soy sauce
2 tbsp malt vinegar
2 tbsp brown sugar
1 tbsp lemon juice
1 cm (½ in) piece fresh ginger,
   finely grated
2 tbsp tomato sauce
2 tbsp water
1 tbsp cornflour
2 tbsp oil

Method

Cut each thigh fillet into 1 cm (½ in)-wide strips. Drain pineapple pieces and reserve the juice. Cut red pepper into strips or squares. Cut spring onions, including most of the green shoot, into 1 cm (½ in) diagonal pieces. Mix together the pineapple juice, soy sauce, vinegar, sugar, lemon juice, ginger and tomato sauce. Blend water and cornflour and set aside.

Heat 2 tablespoons of oil in a wok, then add ⅓ of the chicken. Stir-fry over high heat until cooked, about 1 minute. Remove and cook remaining chicken in 2 batches, adding extra oil if needed. Drain chicken well on absorbent paper. Drain all oil from the wok.

Pour the sauce mixture into the wok and add the blended cornflour. Cook, stirring, until mixture boils and thickens. Stir in red pepper, spring onion and pineapple pieces, cook 1 minute. Add chicken and heat through. Serve immediately with boiled rice.

Chicken Livers With Prawns And Broccoli

Serves 4

Ingredients

250 g (9 oz) chicken livers

2¼ tbsp cornflour

90 g (3½ oz) fresh mushrooms

370 g (13 oz) broccoli

2 tbsp vegetable oil

2 spring onions (scallions),
    chopped finely

125 g (4½ oz) prawns
    (shrimp), peeled

salt

black pepper

1 tbsp soy sauce

5 tbsp water

Method

Trim chicken livers of membranes. Wash and dry, slice thinly and lightly toss in 2 tablespoons of cornflour. Wash and dry mushrooms. Meanwhile, boil broccoli, fresh or frozen, in a pot of salted water for 5 minutes or until al dente.

In a wok or pan, heat oil and fry chicken livers for 90 seconds. Add mushrooms to cook for the same time then add spring onions, drained broccoli and prawns with salt and pepper to taste. Combine well.

Mix remaining cornflour with soy sauce and water until smooth. Add to pan and bring to the boil, stirring until thickened slightly. Cook for a further 2 minutes and serve.

Fragrant Duck with Pineapple

Serves 4

Ingredients

2 boneless Barbary duck breasts,
about 170 g (6 oz) each,
skinned and cut into strips

1 tsp five spice powder

2 tbsp soy sauce

2 tbsp rice wine or dry sherry

1 tsp sugar

1 tbsp peanut oil

1 orange or red pepper
(capsicum), deseeded and cut
into thin strips

5 cm (2 in) piece fresh root
ginger, cut into julienne strips

2 spring onions (scallions),
white and green parts
separated and thinly shredded

170 g (6 oz) fresh pineapple,
cut into bite-sized pieces, plus
juice

salt

Method

Place duck, five spice powder, soy sauce,
rice wine or sherry and sugar in a shallow
non-metallic bowl. Cover and marinate for
20 minutes.

Heat oil in a wok. Remove duck from
marinade and reserve. Stir-fry duck over
a high heat for 2 minutes. Add pepper,
ginger and white spring onions and stir-
fry for a further 3–4 minutes, until pepper
starts to soften.

Add pineapple and juice and the marinade.
Stir-fry for 1–2 minutes. Season with salt
if necessary. Serve straight away, sprinkled
with green spring onions.

Note: Fresh pineapple cuts through
the richness of the tender duck breasts
marinated in Chinese spices. Serve this
dish with plain boiled noodles or some
fragrant Thai rice.

Peking Duck

Serves 6

Ingredients

2 kg (4½ lb) duck
2 tbsp soy sauce
2½ tbsp brown sugar
1 tsp red vinegar

To Serve

hoisin sauce
1 small cucumber, cut into julienne
    strips
6 spring onions (scallions)

Mandarin pancakes

400 g (14 oz) plain flour
pinch of salt
300 ml (10½ fl oz) boiling water
peanut or sesame oil

Method

Plunge duck into a large pot of boiling water for 3 minutes. Drain it, dry it, truss it and hang it up in an airy room to dry completely overnight. Combine soy sauce, brown sugar and vinegar, rub into duck and re-hang for 4 hours. If you can't hang the duck, place on a rack where ventilation is good. Place drip pan beneath.

Place duck on a rack well above a roasting pan half filled with hot water and cook in preheated oven at 190°C (375°F) for 30 minutes. Lower heat, 150°C (300°F) for 1 hour, then adjust to original temperature until skin is crisp and brown all over and the duck is tender.

Cut spring onions to the size of the cucumber strips, about 5 cm (2 in), or for authentic flair, make brushes of the spring onions by cutting them into 7½ cm (3 in) lengths. With a sharp knife, make 2 parallel cuts at each end, about 2½ cm (1 in) deep. Repeat, intersecting these cuts as if drawing a noughts and crosses puzzle. Chill green side down, in iced water until the ends curl.

To make pancakes, sift flour and salt into a bowl. Make a well in the centre, add boiling water and mix to a stiff dough, kneading until smooth. Cover with a damp cloth and leave to rest 15 minutes. On a floured board, shape dough into a roll about 5 cm (2 in) in diameter. Cut the roll into 1 cm (½ in) wide slices to roll into pancakes about 8 cm (3 in) in diameter. Sandwich 2 pancakes together with peanut or sesame oil and roll out pancake pairs to 15 cm (6 in). Repeat. Makes 8 pancakes.

Heat a heavy-based pan on high, but don't let it smoke, before turning it down to a gentle temperature and dry-frying each double pancake for about 1 minute. Pancake should inflate a little and just be slightly marked with brown. When cool enough to touch, separate each pancake and fold in half. To keep pancakes hot while carving duck, cover with foil on a warmed dish.

Carve skin then meat, keeping separate. Arrange on a plate with cucumber. Serve pancakes and spring onion strips or brushes on individual small plates for each diner. Each diner then spreads a little hoisin sauce on the pancakes, tops with some meat then skin, a cucumber matchstick and spring onion to roll up and enjoy.

Meat

Diced Spicy Beef
(Empal Daging)

Serves 4

Ingredients

750 g (1¾ lb) beef, thinly sliced
2 tbsp peanut oil
1 bunch snake beans, trimmed
    into 5 cm (2 in) pieces.
125 ml (4 fl oz) water
Boiled rice, to serve

Paste

1 tsp coriander seeds
3 garlic cloves, chopped
2 tsp galangal, chopped
1 tsp palm sugar or brown sugar
2 tbsp tamarind concentrate
125 ml (4 fl oz) soy sauce

Garnish

Toasted desiccated (dry
    unsweetened shredded)
    coconut

Method

Crush or pound the dry paste ingredients
in a mortar and pestle or food processor.
Crush until a paste has formed. Add
tamarind and soy sauce.

Marinate the beef in the paste in a non-
metallic container for 1–2 hours in the
refrigerator.

Heat oil in a wok. Add beef and stir-fry
for 4–5 minutes. Add beans and cook for
3–4 minutes or until beans are tender.
Add a little water if the sauce is too thick.
Garnish with toasted coconut. Serve with
boiled rice on the side.

Chinese Five Spice Pork Fillet

Serves 6

Ingredients

2 tbsp sunflower or peanut oil

2 small cloves garlic, crushed

2 tbsp Chinese five spice powder

3 tbsp soy sauce

6 tbsp dry or medium sherry

2 spring onions (scallions),
   finely chopped

pared orange rind, cut into strips

juice of 2 large oranges

salt and black pepper

750 g (1¾ lb) pork fillet

15 g (½ oz) butter, chilled and
   cubed

To garnish

fresh snipped chives

Method

In a small bowl, mix together oil, garlic, five spice powder, soy sauce, sherry and spring onions to make a marinade. Add half the orange rind and juice and season with salt and black pepper.

Put pork into a non-metallic bowl, pour the marinade over and cover, or place meat and marinade in a roasting bag, tie bag well and shake. Refrigerate for at least 2 hours, or up to 24 hours, turning the meat or shaking the bag once or twice.

Preheat the oven to 190°C (375°F). Transfer pork fillet and marinade to a roasting tin, loosely cover with foil and cook for 30 minutes. Take off the foil, turn fillet and cook for a further 15 minutes. Cover and leave to stand for 10 minutes. Alternatively, roast in the bag for 45 minutes, then leave to stand for 10 minutes, still in the bag, with the oven door ajar and the heat turned off.

Slice the meat. Pour the cooking juices into a small saucepan, add rest of orange juice and heat gently. Whisk in butter and adjust the seasoning. Serve the slices of meat with the sauce poured over. Garnished with chives and the remaining orange rind.

Beef with Black Bean Sauce

Serves 4

Ingredients

500 g (1 lb 2 oz) sirloin or
 rump steak, cut into thin
 strips
1 clove garlic, crushed
1 small red chilli, deseeded and
 finely chopped (optional)
1 tbsp dark soy sauce
black pepper
2 tsp cornflour
1 tbsp water
1 tbsp white wine vinegar
2 tbsp vegetable oil
1 yellow and 1 red pepper
 (capsicum), deseeded and cut
 into strips
1 large zucchini (courgette), cut
 into julienned strips
150 g (5 oz) snow peas, sliced
3 tbsp black bean stir-fry sauce
4 spring onions (scallions),
 sliced

Method

Combine steak strips, garlic, chilli (if
using), soy sauce and pepper in a bowl. In
another bowl, mix cornflour with water
until smooth, then stir in vinegar.

Heat oil in a wok or large frying pan until
very hot. Add meat and its marinade
and stir-fry for 4 minutes, tossing
continuously, until meat is seared on
all sides.

Add peppers and stir-fry for 2 minutes.
Stir in the zucchini and snow peas and
cook for 3 minutes. Reduce the heat and
add cornflour mixture and black bean
sauce. Stir to mix thoroughly, then cook
for 2 minutes or until meat and vegetables
are cooked through. Scatter with spring
onions just before serving. If desired, serve
over egg noodles cooked according to
packet directions.

Sizzling Beef

Serves 4

Ingredients

500 g (1 lb 2 oz) rump steak,
    trimmed of any excess fat and
    cut into thin strips

2 tbsp soy sauce

2 tbsp rice wine or sherry

1½ tbsp cornflour

1 tsp sugar

3 tbsp peanut oil

150 g (5 oz) broccoli, cut into
    bite-size pieces

1 large red pepper (capsicum),
    deseeded and cut into thin
    strips

2 cloves garlic, crushed

3 tbsp oyster sauce

200 g (7 oz) pack fresh bean
    sprouts

salt and black pepper

Method

Put steak, soy sauce, rice wine or sherry, cornflour and sugar into a non-metallic bowl and mix thoroughly.

Heat 1 tablespoon of oil in a wok or large heavy-based frying-pan, add one third of the beef mixture and stir-fry over a high heat for 2–3 minutes until browned. Remove and cook remaining beef in 2 more batches, adding a little more oil if necessary.

Heat remaining oil in wok, then add broccoli and 6 tablespoons of water. Stir-fry for 5 minutes, then add pepper and garlic and stir-fry for a further 2–3 minutes, until the broccoli is tender but still firm to the bite.

Stir in oyster sauce, return the beef to the wok and add bean sprouts. Toss over a high heat for 2 minutes or until beef is piping hot and bean sprouts have softened slightly. Add salt and pepper to taste.

Sweet and Sour Pork

Serves 6

Ingredients

400 g (14 oz) lean pork, cubed
pinch of salt
½ tsp ground black pepper
2 tbsp dry sherry
1 egg, lightly beaten
4 tbsp cornflour
vegetable oil for frying

Sauce

½ carrot, cut in julienne strips
1 small green pepper (capsicum)
4 spring onions (scallions),
    chopped
1 fresh red chilli, seeded and
    finely chopped
2 cloves garlic, crushed
1 tsp fresh ginger, grated
3 tbsp tomato sauce or 1 tbsp
    tomato paste
1 tbsp soy sauce
3 tbsp honey
1 tbsp cornflour
1 small can pineapple pieces,
    drained and juice reserved
vegetable oil for frying

Method

Prepare vegetables for sauce. Core, seed and cut pepper into thin rings and cut each ring in half. Put pork cubes in a bowl, sprinkle with salt and pepper, add sherry, mix and marinate for 30 minutes.

Toss pork cubes in a bag containing cornflour then dip pork in beaten egg and toss in cornflour again. Heat some oil in a preheated wok or heavy-based pan and deep-fry pork until brown. Drain on paper towels and reserve.

Drain off all oil except for about 2 tablespoons, heat and add spring onions, pepper, chilli, garlic and ginger and stir-fry for 2 minutes. Mix tomato sauce or paste, soy sauce, honey, cornflour and juice from pineapple. When smooth, add to wok and stir until thickened. Add water if too thick. Stir in pork and drained pineapple pieces, heat through and serve.

Note: Pork chops, pre-cooked meatballs of any sort, chicken, uncooked peeled prawns, and pieces of white fish also team very well with the sauce.

Seafood

Sambal Fried Prawns (Udang Goreng)

Serves 4

Ingredients

1 tbsp vegetable oil

24 green prawns (shrimp), heads and shells removed

Nasi goreng (see recipe page 127), to serve

Plain rice, to serve (optional)

Paste

3 garlic cloves, chopped

3 medium chillies, deseeded and chopped

3 tsp root ginger, chopped

1 stalk lemongrass, chopped

1 tsp ground coriander

Pinch of salt

2 tsp vegetable oil

Method

Crush or pound the paste ingredients in a mortar with a pestle or use a food processor.

Heat the oil in a wok or frying pan. Add the prawns and paste, and stir-fry for 3–4 minutes, or until cooked.

Serve with nasi goreng or plain rice.

Baked Fish with Spicy Soy Sauce (Ikan Kecap)

Serves 4

Ingredients

800 g–1 kg (1¾ lb–2 lb) whole
  snapper
2 tsp peanut oil
1 tbsp lemon juice
Pinch of salt
Lemon slices
Boiled rice, to serve

Sauce

2 tsp peanut oil
2 garlic cloves, crushed
2 tsp root ginger, grated
  (crushed)
1 small red chilli, deseeded and
  sliced
4 spring onions (scallions),
  sliced
2 tbsp soy sauce
1 tbsp sweet soy sauce (kecap
  manis)
125 ml (4 fl oz) water

Method

Preheat the oven to 200°C (400°F).

Make two diagonal cuts on each side of
the fish, then brush with oil and lemon
juice. Season with salt and place slices of
lemon in the fish. Wrap the fish in baking
paper and aluminium foil and place on a
baking sheet. Bake in preheated oven for
30–40 minutes or until cooked.

To make the sauce, heat the oil in a small
saucepan. Add the garlic, ginger, chilli and
spring onions and cook for 1–2 minutes.
Add the soy sauce, kecap manis and water
and cook for 2–3 minutes.

When the fish is cooked, transfer it to a
large serving dish and pour the sauce over.
Serve with side bowls of boiled rice.

Pan-Fried Fish
(Ikan Goreng)

Serves 4

Ingredients

4 boneless fish fillets

1 tbsp peanut oil

250 ml (8 fl oz) coconut milk

1 tsp palm sugar or brown sugar

1 tbsp lemon juice

4 spring onions (scallions),
   sliced

Paste

2 garlic cloves, chopped

2 tsp root ginger, chopped

1 stalk lemongrass, sliced

2 medium chillies, deseeded and
   sliced

2 candle nuts

1 tsp shrimp paste (terasi)

1 tsp ground coriander

2 tsp peanut oil

Method

Grind or pound the paste ingredients
in a mortar with a pestle, or use a food
processor. Brush the paste over the
fish fillets.

Heat the peanut oil in a large frying
pan. Add the fish fillets and cook for
1–2 minutes on each side. Add the coconut
milk, sugar and lemon juice and simmer
for 2–3 minutes. Serve the fish topped
with spring onions.

Marinated Barbecue Seafood (Udang Cumi-Cumi Bakar)

Serves 4

Ingredients

Bamboo skewers, soaked in water for 15 minutes

60 ml (2 fl oz) peanut oil

Zest of 2 limes, grated

75 ml (3 fl oz) lime juice

3 medium chillies, deseeded and finely chopped

3 garlic cloves, crushed

400 g (14 oz) squid, cut into pieces

16 large green prawns (shrimp), shells removed

500 g (1 lb 2 oz) baby octopus, cleaned and trimmed

Boiled rice, to serve

Method

Combine the oil, lime zest and juice, chillies and garlic in a shallow dish. Score the inside skin of the squid diagonally in both directions.

Thread the prawns lengthways onto bamboo skewers and brush the marinade over them. Add the squid pieces and octopus and brush with marinade. Leave to marinate in a refrigerator for 30 minutes.

Cook the skewers on a barbecue plate, or chargrill for 5–10 minutes, or until cooked. Serve with side bowls of boiled rice.

Fish in Banana Leaves
(Ikan Panggang)

Serves 4

Ingredients

8 pieces banana leaf or kitchen foil

750 g (1¾ lb) boneless white fish fillets, diced

2 shallots, chopped

2 garlic cloves, chopped

1 tbsp root ginger, chopped

¼ tsp ground turmeric

2 tsp ground coriander (cilantro)

75 ml (3 fl oz) coconut milk

Juice of 1 lime

Salt, to taste

4 medium red chillies, deseeded and sliced

4 lime leaves, shredded

Lime wedges, to serve

Method

Prepare the banana leaves by cutting into 15 cm (6 in) square pieces. Dip each leaf in a bowl of bowling water.

Combine the fish, shallots, garlic, ginger, turmeric, coriander, coconut milk, lime juice and salt in a food processor. Process until the mixture comes together.

Divide the mixture evenly into 8 and place in the middle of each banana leaf. Top with chilli and lime leaves. Fold banana leaf over fish, flatten a little and secure ends with cocktail sticks.

Cook the fish on a barbecue for 3 minutes on each side, or cook in a steamer for 3–4 minutes. Serve with wedges of lime.

Sambal Fried Snapper (Sambal Ikan Goreng)

Serves 4

Ingredients

1 tsp ground cumin

1 tsp ground coriander

Zest of 1 lime, grated (shredded)

2 tbsp lime juice

Salt, to taste

4 small snapper

40 g (1½ oz) plain (all-purpose) flour

Peanut oil, for cooking

Marinade

2 shallots, chopped

2 garlic cloves, chopped

2 tsp root ginger, chopped

2 medium chillies, deseeded and sliced

Method

Grind or pound the marinade ingredients in a mortar with a pestle, or use a food processor. Add the cumin, coriander, zest and lime juice and salt to the marinade.

Make two slits on each side of the snapper. Brush the mixture over the fish and marinate for 1 hour in the refrigerator. Dip the fish in the flour.

Heat the oil in a wok or large frying pan. Fry the fish for 2–3 minutes on each side, or until crisp on the outside and cooked through. Serve with the sambals (sauces) of your choice.

Spicy Fish Fritters
(Perkedel Ikan)

Makes about 16

Ingredients

4 spring onions (scallions),
    sliced
2 garlic cloves, chopped
2 tsp root ginger, chopped
500 g (1 lb 2 oz) boneless fish
    fillets
1 tbsp soy sauce
2 tsp sweet soy sauce (kecap
    manis)
1 egg
1 tbsp cornflour (corn starch)
Peanut oil, for cooking

Dipping sauce

1 tbsp sweet soy sauce
2 tbsp soy sauce
½ tsp sambal oelek

Method

Combine the shallots, garlic, ginger, fish, soy sauce, kecap manis, egg and cornflour in a food processor. Process until the mixture comes together and is smooth.

Using wet hands shape the mixture into small patties (the mixture tends to be wet) and put on a plate. Cover with cling film (plastic wrap) and let stand for 30 minutes to 1 hour in the refrigerator.

Heat the oil in a non-stick frying pan or wok. Cook the patties for 1–2 minutes on each side, or until golden.

Combine the ingredients for dipping sauce in a small dish. Serve the fritters with dipping sauce.

Chinese-Style Steamed Grey Mullet

Serves 2

Ingredients

1 grey mullet, about 700 g (1lb 8oz), scaled, gutted and cleaned

½ tsp salt

1 tbsp vegetable oil

1 tbsp light soy sauce

1 large carrot, cut into fine strips

4 spring onions (scallions), cut into fine strips

1 tbsp fresh root ginger, grated

1 tbsp sesame oil (optional)

To garnish

fresh coriander (cilantro) leaves

Method

Make 4 deep slashes along each side of the fish, then rub the fish inside and out with salt, vegetable oil and soy sauce. Cover and place in the refrigerator for 30 minutes.

Spread half the carrot, spring onions and ginger on a large piece of foil. Place fish on top, then sprinkle with remaining vegetables and ginger and any remaining marinade. Loosely fold over foil to seal. Transfer fish to a steamer. Alternatively, transfer to a plate, then place on a rack in oven at 200°C (400°F) set over a roasting tin half filled with water. Cover tightly with a lid or with foil.

Cook for 20 minutes or until the fish is firm and cooked through. Put sesame oil, if using, into a small saucepan and heat. Drizzle over fish and garnish with coriander.

Cantonese Spicy Squid

Serves 4

Ingredients

500 g (1 lb 2 oz) squid
1 tsp ginger juice
1 tbsp dry sherry
725 ml (1¼ pint) water
a pinch of five spice powder
½ tsp salt
2 tsp ground white pepper
vegetable oil
½ small green pepper
   (capsicum), seeded and sliced
   into rings

Method

Remove and discard squid heads, backbones and ink sacs. Wash and dry on kitchen paper. Slit open squid tubes, flatten and score inside meat in a criss-cross pattern with a sharp-pointed knife.

Squeeze ginger juice from whole pieces of peeled ginger root using a garlic press. Cut squid into 3cm squares. In a bowl, combine ginger juice and sherry and marinate squid squares for 45 minutes.

Boil water and, in a bowl, immerse squid for several seconds until criss-cross patterns turn into bumps. Drain off water and dry squid thoroughly on kitchen paper.

Deep-fry squid in vegetable oil on medium heat for no more than 20 seconds. Drain on kitchen paper and sprinkle with combined salt, pepper and five spice powder, turning to cover each piece. Spoon onto serving plate. Garnish with rings of pepper.

Shellfish Custard

Serves 4

Ingredients

500 g (1 lb 2 oz) clams or
    mussels in shells
3 spring onions (scallions),
    sliced
2 tsp fresh ginger, crushed
oil for frying
6 egg whites, beaten well
3 eggs
400 ml (14 fl oz) stock
2 tbsp cornflour
½ tsp salt
½ tsp ground black pepper
1 tbsp dry sherry
lemon wedges and parsley to
    garnish

Method

De-beard clams or mussels and gently scrub shells before thoroughly rinsing in water. Dry and, with spring onions and ginger, place in oil in a wok or pan on medium heat and cover. Remove shells when most have opened, having shaken the pan occasionally to aid this. Discard any shells which have not opened.

Remove shellfish meat and place in a serving dish which fits on top of a saucepan for steaming. To make custard, gently mix egg whites with whole eggs and chicken stock smoothly blended with cornflour. Add salt, black pepper and sherry. Add mixture to shellfish in dish.

Place dish on top of saucepan and steam over quickly boiling water until custard is set. Serve with lemon wedges and garnish with parsley. Serve in dish or, alternatively, steam and serve in individual heatproof mini soufflé dishes.

Chinese Lobster Stir-Fry

Serves 4

Ingredients

500 g (1 lb 2 oz) lobster meat,
   fresh or frozen

1 small clove garlic, minced

2 tbsp oil

125 ml (4 fl oz) chicken broth

1 small red pepper (capsicum)

250 g (9 oz) bean sprouts

250 g (9 oz) water chestnuts

250 g (9 oz) broccoli

370 g (13 oz) Chinese cabbage,
   chopped

½ tsp salt

¼ tsp pepper

1 egg, beaten

rice to serve

Method

If frozen, thaw and chop lobster meat into bite-size pieces. In a skillet sauté lobster and garlic in oil for 1 minute. Add broth and vegetables and simmer, uncovered, for 5 minutes. Season with salt and pepper.

Add a little of the hot broth to lightly beaten egg. Stir the egg mixture into the rest of the broth. Heat gently but do not boil. Serve with rice.

Sushi and Sashimi

Equipment

This is a basic set of utensils for making sushi.

Rice-cooling tub (hangiri)

Used for cooling the vinegared rice giving it the perfect texture and gloss. It is made of cypress bound with copper hoops, but any wooden or plastic vessel can be used instead.

Spatula (shamoji)

Used to turn and spread sushi rice while cooling it. Traditionally the spatula is a symbol of the housewife's position in the household. You can use an ordinary spoon instead, wooden or plastic.

Fan (uchiwa)

Used to drive off moisture to get the right texture and flavor of sushi rice. Originally this fan was made of bamboo ribs covered with either paper or silk. If no fan is available, a piece of cardboard or a magazine can be used instead.

Bowl

A large bowl with a lid is necessary to keep the cooked sushi rice warm while making your sushi.

Chopping board (manaita)

This is a must. Traditionally made of wood, but nowadays many people prefer chopping boards made of rubber or resin, as these are easier to keep clean.

Chopsticks (saibashi)

There are two types of chopsticks: long chopsticks for cooking, often made from metal, and shorter chopsticks for eating.

Tweezers

Used to remove small bones from fish. Larger, straight-ended tweezers are better than the smaller variety commonly found in the bathroom and can be obtained from fish markets or specialty stores.

Rolling mat (makisu)

Made of bamboo woven together with cotton string, this is used to make rolled sushi.

Knives

The only way to get nicely cut surfaces is to use steel knives of good quality. Use whetstones to sharpen the blades yourself. Good Japanese knives are an outgrowth of forging the Japanese sword which is world famous for its sharpness. The knives are a chef's most valuable possessions and sushi chefs keep a wet cloth nearby, frequently wiping the blades to keep their knives clean as they work. Here are the basic types:

Cleavers (deba-bocho).

Wide heavy knives with triangular-shaped blades capable of cutting bone.

Vegetable knives (nakiri-bocho).

Lighter than cleavers, these have rectangular blades.

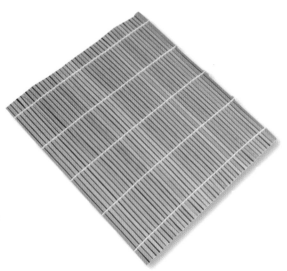

Fish knives (sashimi-bocho).

Long and slender, with the pointed type being most popular in Osaka and the blunt-ended type most popular in Tokyo. Excellent for filleting and slicing fish, they are also just right for slicing rolled sushi.

Ingredients

Vinegar

Sugared water or any alcoholic beverage, allowed to stand long enough, naturally sours and becomes vinegar. The word in itself is French and comes from vin (wine) and *aigre* (sour). In Japan it is made from rice, the grain from which sake is brewed. With the power to alter proteins, vinegar destroys bacteria. Adding sugar to sushi rice is to prevent the tartness of vinegar from coming through too strongly.

Soy Sauce

Soy sauce is popular all over the world, used under many appellations: all flavor, meat sauce, all-purpose seasoning, etc. Japanese soy sauce, rather than the darker and richer Chinese variety, is the one for sushi lovers. Soy sauce is highly recommended as a natural fermented food, superior to salt, sugar or synthetic seasonings. It is essential to most traditional Japanese foods, including sushi, tempura, sukiyaki and noodles.

To tell good soy sauce from bad, use the following guidelines:

Aroma. A good soy sauce never produces an unpleasant smell, no matter how deeply you inhale.

Color. When a small quantity is poured into a white dish, good soy sauce looks reddish.

Clarity. Good soy sauce is perfectly translucent.

Sunlight passing through it gives it a lovely glow.

Once opened, soy sauce should be stored in a cool, dark, dry place or refrigerated.

Pickled Ginger (gari or shoga)

Ginger is used to cleanse the palate between bites of sushi. It does not take a lot of ginger to cleanse the palate, so that a small pile should be enough for several rolls. Pickled ginger can be bought in Asian food stores, but if you wish to make your own, try this recipe.

ingredients:

250 g (9 oz) fresh ginger
90 ml (3 fl oz) rice vinegar
2 tbsp/25 ml mirin
2 tbsp/25 ml sake
5 tsp/25 ml sugar

Method

Scrub the ginger under running water. Blanch in boiling water for one minute, drain and cut into medium-sized pieces.

Combine rice vinegar, mirin, sake and sugar in a small pan. Bring to a boil, stirring until the sugar has dissolved. Cool.

Place the ginger in a sterilized jar and pour the cooled vinegar over it. Cover and keep 3–4 days before using. Will keep refrigerated for up to one month.

Although the pale pink color develops as it ages, you might want to add a small amount of red food coloring.5 Slice thinly before serving.

Nori (Seaweed)

After harvesting, this seaweed is dried, toasted and sold packaged in standard size sheets (7½x8½in/19x21cm). Once the sealed cellophane or plastic bag has been opened, nori should be eaten at once or stored in a sealed container in a dry, cool, dark place to preserve its crispiness. Nori is particularly rich in vitamins A, B12 and D. Nori belts are used on nigiri-sushi when the topping being used is likely to slip off the rice, such as omelet and tofu.

Tezu

A bowl of half sushi vinegar and half water, used to wet hands, knife, seal nori rolls, etc., making it easier to handle sushi rice and toppings.

Sake

A colorless brewed alcoholic beverage made from rice, legally defined as a rice beer. Its bouquet is somewhat earthy, with subtle undertones; it has a slightly sweet initial taste, followed by a dry aftertaste. Sake should be stored in a cool, dark place prior to opening, then in the refrigerator after opening. Very popular in Japan, it is the traditional drink served before eating sushi, and should be served warm.

Mirin

Mirin is known as sweet sake, and is generally only used for seasoning. If unavailable, sweet sherry makes a suitable substitute.

Ingredients

Daikon radish

A Japanese white radish, available fresh in Asian stores, in sizes ranging from 15 cm (6 in) to 90 cm (3 ft). It may be refrigerated for several weeks. Cut into very fine slivers, it is commonly eaten with sashimi and can be used as a substitute for nori seaweed. When it is minced, it can be added to soy sauce for different texture and flavor.

Tofu

Custard-like cake of soybean curd, about 8 cm (3 in) square. Sold fresh in supermarkets, it will keep for several days if refrigerated submerged in fresh water. Tofu is used in nigiri-sushi as a substitute for sushi rice, or as a topping on the rice.

Sushi Rice

When it comes to sushi, the rice is as important as the fish, and it takes years of training to learn how to make perfect sushi rice. There are different ways of doing it, but by following the directions on page 182–183 you will have a universally accepted and uncomplicated method of making the rice.

Sesame seeds

White sesame seeds are roasted and used as an aromatic seasoning, while black seeds are mostly used as a garnish.

Wasabi

Grown only in Japan, wasabi horseradish, when grated finely, is a pungent, refreshing pulp that removes unpleasant fishiness. Fresh wasabi is very expensive and difficult to obtain, so the best alternative is the powdered variety. Mix it with water to get a firm consistency. The wasabi purchased in tubes tends to be too strong and lacks that real wasabi flavor.

Mayonnaise

Not extensively used in sushi cooking, with the notable exception of the California roll.

Instead of using the standard commercially-made egg mayonnaise, try this homemade variety with a slight Japanese influence.

ingredients:

3 egg yolks
½ tsp/2 ml lemon juice
60 ml (2 fl oz) white miso
250 ml (8 fl oz) vegetable oil
salt to taste
sprinkle of white pepper
a pinch of grated yuzu, lime, or lemon peel

Method

In a bowl, beat the egg yolks and lemon juice with a wooden spoon.

Continue to beat, adding the vegetable oil a few drops at a time until the mixture begins to emulsify. Keep on adding the rest of the oil.

Stir in the miso and the seasonings.

Refrigerate before using.

Note: Yuzu is a Japanese orange used only for its rind. Kaffir lime used in Thai or Malaysian food is an alternative, as is lemon or lime rind.

Nigiri-Sushi with Prawns (Ebi)

Makes 10 pieces

Ingredients

10 thin bamboo skewers, 15 cm
    (6 in) long
10 green king prawns
475 ml (16 fl oz) water
1 tsp/5 ml salt
1 tsp/5 ml vinegar

vinegar water:

475 ml (16 fl oz) water
250 ml (8 fl oz) vinegar

475 ml (16 fl oz) sushi rice
    (see page 182–183)
2 tsp/10 ml wasabi

Method

Insert a bamboo skewer through each
prawn to prevent curling.

Drop the prawns into a saucepan holding
475 ml (16 fl oz) of boiling water and
the salt and vinegar, and simmer for
2–3 minutes.

Scoop out prawns and drop them into
ice water. Refresh with more cold water
if necessary to ensure prawns are well
chilled.

Twist skewers to remove prawns. Then
shell prawns removing the legs and head
but leaving the tips of the tails intact.

To remove the vein, slice lengthwise along
the back and pull vein out.

Insert the knife along the leg side of the
prawn and open like a butterfly.

Soak in salted water for 20 minutes. Then
transfer into a bowl containing the vinegar
water and soak for a further 20 minutes.

Proceed to make nigiri-sushi as described
on pages 184–185.

Nigiri-Sushi with Salmon (Sake)

Makes 20 pieces

Ingredients

300 g (10½ oz) salmon fillet
475 ml (16 fl oz) sushi rice
    (see page 182–183)
1 tbsp/15 ml wasabi

Method

Using the flat or angled cut, slice the fillet thinly.

Proceed using the nigiri-sushi making techinique on pages 184–185.

Nigiri-Sushi with Tuna (Maguru)

Makes 20 pieces

Ingredients:

300 g (10½ oz) tuna fillet
475 ml (16 fl oz) sushi rice
   (see pages 182–183)
1 tbsp/15 ml wasabi

Method

Slice the fillet using the flat or angled cut.

Proceed using the nigiri-sushi making techinique on pages 184–185.

Note: Several different varieties of tuna are available at the fish market and to the fisherman. The 4 recommended types of tuna are:

Bluefin tuna — considered by most Japanese to be the superior fish in the tuna family.

Bigeye tuna — also highly regarded, exceeded in price on the Japanese markets only by the bluefin tuna.

Yellowfin tuna — an extremely important and widely resourced tropical tuna.

Albacore — well regarded for sashimi, but quite high in calories. Often refered to as "chicken of the sea" with its slight chicken flavor when cooked.

Opposite: Salmon, prawn and tuna sushi

Chirashi Sushi with Tofu

Makes 15-20 pieces

The easiest type of sushi to make, made in all Japanese kitchens, is chirashi, or scattered, sushi. Chirashi-sushi is simply sushi rice with other ingredients mixed in or placed on the top. Chirashi-sushi without any seafood often makes its appearance in lunch boxes. It's taken on picnics and often sold on railway station platforms. Station lunches are not exclusively chirashi-sushi but many are. Stations are known for their type of food as well as for the unique containers in which they package their lunches. Again, the variations of this type of sushi are almost limitless. The rice can also be seasoned with a range of interesting ingredients such as chopped vegetables, sesame seeds, tofu pieces, chopped fresh and pickled ginger, crumbled nori and a variety of sauces.

Ingredients:

300 g (10½ oz) tofu
    (substitute for sushi rice)
grated ginger
chopped shallot
1 tsp/5 ml soy sauce
assortment of various fish,
meat and vegetables
15–20 nori belts

Suggestions for toppings:

tuna
prawns
omelet
cuttlefish
salmon
unagi eel
yellowtail
bonito
avocado
tofu
crab
vegetables

Method

Cut the tofu into nigiri-sized pieces.

Mix the ginger, shallot and soy sauce.

Prepare topping ingredients.

Place the topping onto the tofu and tie with nori belts (see page 101).

Put the mixed ginger on top then serve.

Note: The garnish already contains soy, so a bowl of soy and wasabi is not necessary.

Opposite: Tofu Sushi, with (L-R) seared beef, pickled yellowtail and smoked salmon

Maki-Sushi ...

Maki-sushi is a "rolled sushi". Maki means
wrapping, and maki-sushi is narrow strips
of different ingredients layered on a bed of
vinegared rice all wrapped up with a sheet
of nori or seaweed. Maki-sushi is the most
well-known and varied sushi because just
about any ingredient can be rolled into the
center, from seafood to crisp vegetables,
pickles, strips of omelet or avocado.

Cucumber Rolls (Kappamaki)

Makes 24 pieces

Ingredients

4 pieces cucumber, each cut as ½ x 1 x 7½ cm (¼ x ½ x 3 in) strips

2 sheets nori (cut in half)

250 ml (8 fl oz) sushi rice (see page 182–183)

1 tsp/5 ml wasabi

Method

Slice cucumber into strips.

Proceed to make cucumber rolls as described on pages 186–187.

Note: You can further your variations by using ingredients such as fresh salmon, smoked salmon, prawns, avocado, minced tuna with chili, omelet and umeboshi plums instead of the cucumber.

Tuna Rolls (Tekkamaki)

Makes 24 pieces

Ingredients

2 nori sheets (cut in half)

250 ml (8 fl oz) sushi rice (see page 182–183)

4 pieces tuna, each cut as ½ x 1 x 7½ cm (¼ x ½ x 3 in) strips

1 tsp/5 ml wasabi

Method

Slice tuna into strips.

Proceed to make tuna rolls as described on pages 186–187.

Thin Sushi Rolls (Hosomaki)

Before making a sushi roll cut the nori in half, then cut the sheets so they have straight sides. The scraps can be used as nori belts.

California Rolls
(Ura Makisushi)

Makes 24 pieces

Ingredients

4 medium cooked prawns or
    seafood sticks
1 ripe avocado, peeled, seeded
    and sliced
1 cucumber, cut into thin slices
8 tsp/40 ml flying fish roe
4–8 leaf lettuce leaves
2 nori sheets (cut in half)
750 ml (1½ pt) sushi rice
    (see page 182–183)
1 tbsp/15 ml wasabi
3 tbsp/45 ml Japanese
    mayonnaise

Method

Shell and de-vein prawns, slice in half lengthwise. Slice avocado and cucumber.

Make California rolls as described on pages 189–190.

Variations: Clean one large carrot, cut in thick strips and blanch. In salt water, blanch 90 g (30 oz) English spinach, rinse in cold water, drain and shake dry. Cut 90 g (30 oz) fresh salmon fillet in finger thick slices and marinate in mirin. Prepare the California roll as described.

Temaki Sushi

Makes 10 pieces

Temaki sushi originally was a meal for busy chefs. Having the ingredients on hand but no time to make sushi for themselves, they created this hand-roll sushi. Temaki offers a good way to experiment with ingredients such as cooked chicken, raw or rare beef and flavorsome sauces. They are quick and easy to prepare and taste delicious, even with an inexpensive filling. Small Temaki Sushi are perfect as an appetizer because they are easy to eat as finger food.

· If you cannot buy roasted nori sheets, you can roast them yourself. Lightly toast one side of the sheet of nori for about 30 seconds over a gas flame. Or toast them in a frying pan without oil on low heat until the aroma comes out. The nori will be crisp and have a dark green color after cooking. Leftovers from roasted nori sheets can be chopped and used as a seasoning or snack.

· If you make Temaki Sushi with soft or semi-liquid ingredients, it is easier with the rice at the bottom and the filling above it.

· Daikon radish sprouts are a popular ingredient for Temaki and Maki-Sushi and go well with omelet sushi. They resemble large mustard and cress, but are much hotter and spicier. Buy them in Asian supermarkets.

Ingredients

5 nori sheets, halved
750 ml (1½ pt) sushi rice
   (see page 182–183)
wasabi

Suggestions for Fillings

tuna slices
spicy tuna
tempura prawns
teriyaki chicken
cooked prawns
crab sticks
unagi eel fillets
pickled whiting or yellowtail
   sashimi
flying fish, salmon or sea urchin roe
omelet
cucumber
avocado
smoked salmon (or any smoked fish)
instead of wasabi, try Japanese
   mayonnaise or cream cheese

Follow instructions on page 188.

Note: As an unusual variation or in case you run out of nori sheets, temaki sushi may even be rolled in lettuce, particularly cos (romaine) or iceberg. Lettuce makes a light, refreshing roll.

Tuna Sashimi (Maguro)

Ingredients

300 g (10½ oz) sashimi-grade
    tuna fillet
tosa juya (dipping sauce):
3 tbsp/45 ml soy sauce
2½ tsp/12 ml sake
5 tsp/25 ml dried bonito
    (katsuobushi)

Method

Proceed to cut tuna into flat cuts.

To make Tosa Juya, put soy sauce, sake and dried bonito into a small saucepan and bring to the boil, stirring constantly, for 2 minutes.

Strain through a fine sieve and cool to room temperature. Divide dipping sauce among small dishes and serve with tuna sashimi.

Note: If the fillet you have purchased has already been cut into a block, you can proceed to cut the fish into the sashimi. If, on the other hand, the fillet has not been trimmed and shaped into a block, then you may need to buy a larger fillet and trim it down to size yourself, perhaps using the off-cuts as minced tuna.

Salmon Sashimi (Sake)

Ingredients

300 g (10½ oz) sashimi-grade salmon or 1 whole salmon

shredded daikon radish

Method

If purchasing a whole salmon, proceed to clean, gut and fillet the fish.

Trim away any dark or bruised flesh that may be evident, as well as any skin and fatty flesh.

Shape the fillets into a block and apply the flat cut, cutting off required number of pieces. (Any off-cuts of salmon may be minced, mixed with wasabi and used in Battleship Sushi).

Arrange on plate and garnish with shredded daikon radish.

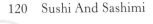

Side dishes

Green Beans with Soy Sauce (Buncis Kecap)

Serves 4

Ingredients

1 tbsp peanut oil

1 tsp sesame oil

1 garlic clove, crushed

2 shallots, sliced

300 g (10½ oz) green (French) beans, trimmed and halved

2 tbsp soy sauce

2 tbsp water

115 g (4 oz) beansprouts, trimmed

40 g (1½ oz) roasted peanuts, chopped

Method

Heat the oil in a wok or frying pan. Add the sesame oil, garlic, shallots and beans. Stir-fry for 2–3 minutes. Add the soy sauce and water and cook for 3–4 minutes, or until the beans are just cooked. Stir through the beansprouts and peanuts. Serve warm or cold.

Fried Rice (Nasi Goreng)

Serves 6

Ingredients

400 g (14 oz) long-grain rice, rinsed

1½ tbsp peanut oil

2 eggs, lightly beaten

4 green shallots, finely sliced

2 garlic cloves, crushed

2 small red chillies, deseeded and finely chopped

300 g (10½ oz) chicken thigh fillets, diced

1 carrot, finely sliced or grated

225 g (8 oz) shredded Chinese cabbage

100 g (3½ oz) prawns (shrimp), peeled and cooked

2–3 tbsp sweet soy sauce (kecap manis)

1 tbsp soy sauce

Method

Cook the rice in boiling salted water for 10–12 minutes, or until cooked. Drain and rinse.

Heat 2 teaspoons of the oil in a wok. Add the egg and swirl to coat the wok to form an omelette. Flip the omelette and cook the other side. Remove and cut into thin strips.

Heat the remaining oil in wok. Add the green shallots, garlic and chilli and cook for 1–2 minutes. Add the chicken and stir-fry for 3 minutes. Add the carrot, cabbage, prawns, kecap manis and soy sauce and stir-fry until the cabbage wilts.

Add the rice to the mixture and stir-fry until heated through. Serve rice with strips of omelette, fried shallots and the sambal (sauce) of your choice.

This dish can be served as a meal with chicken satay and garnished with a fried egg. Ingredients in rice can vary to suit your taste. If serving with meats you can omit the chicken and prawns.

Spicy Snake Beans (Sambal Buncis)

Serves 4

Ingredients

2 tsp peanut oil

125 ml (4 fl oz) chicken stock

1 stalk lemongrass, bruised

250 g (9 oz) snake beans
   (Chinese long beans),
   trimmed

Paste

2 medium red chillies, deseeded
   and sliced

2 shallots, chopped

2 tsp root ginger, chopped

2 tsp garlic, chopped

Vegetable oil (optional)

Method

Grind or pound the paste ingredients in a mortar with a pestle, or use a small food processor. If using a food processor you may need to add a little oil.

Heat the peanut oil in a wok or frying pan. Add the paste and cook for 1–2 minutes. Add the stock and lemongrass. Bring to the boil. Add the beans and cook for 8–10 minutes, or until the beans are tender.

Note: Asian greens can be used instead of beans.

Carrots and Snowpeas with Sesame Seeds

Serves 4

Ingredients

½ cucumber

2 tbsp sesame seeds

1 tbsp sunflower oil

4 carrots, cut into matchsticks

225 g (8 oz) snowpeas

6 spring onions (scallions),
   chopped

1 tbsp lemon juice

black pepper

Method

Peel the cucumber, cut it in half lengthwise and scoop out the seeds. Slice into half moons.

Heat a non-stick wok or large frying pan. Add the sesame seeds and dry-fry for 1 minute or until toasted, tossing constantly. Remove and set aside. Add the oil, then the cucumber and carrots and stir-fry over a high heat for 2 minutes. Add the snowpeas and spring onions and stir-fry for a further 2–3 minutes, until all the vegetables are cooked but still crisp.

Sprinkle over the lemon juice and sesame seeds, toss to mix and stir-fry for a few seconds to heat through. Season with pepper and serve.

Vegetarian

Spicy Fried Tempeh (Sambal Goreng Tempe)

Serves 4

Ingredients

125 ml (4 fl oz) peanut oil

300 g (10½ oz) tempeh, cut into thin strips

2 tsp peanut oil, extra

2 cloves garlic, crushed

½ tsp shrimp paste (terasi)

1 tbsp tamarind concentrate

2 tbsp soy sauce

1 tsp palm sugar or brown sugar

2 tbsp water

2 spring onions (scallions), sliced

1 medium red chilli, deseeded and sliced

Method

Heat the peanut oil in a wok or frying pan. Cook the tempeh in batches until golden and crisp. Remove and set aside.

Heat the extra oil, garlic and shrimp paste and cook for 30 seconds. Add the tamarind, soy sauce, sugar, water and tempeh. Cook until the sauce has reduced.

Garnish with sliced spring onions and chillies. Serve as a main or side dish.

Fried Noodles (Bakmi Goreng)

Serves 4

Ingredients

200 g (7 oz) dried egg noodles
  or thin noodles

1 tbsp peanut oil

4 shallots, sliced

500 g (1 lb 2 oz) chicken thigh
  fillets, diced

2 garlic cloves, crushed

1 carrot, peeled and finely sliced
  or grated (shredded)

225 g (8 oz) Chinese cabbage,
  shredded

2 tbsp sweet soy sauce (kecap
  manis)

75 ml (3 fl oz) chicken stock

115 g (4 oz) beansprouts

4 spring onions (scallions),
  sliced

Method

Cook the noodles following the packet directions. Drain and set aside.

Heat the oil in a wok. Add the shallots and cook until golden. Add the chicken and garlic and stir-fry until just cooked. Add carrots and stir-fry for another 2 minutes. Add the cabbage, kecap manis and stock and continue to cook until the cabbage is wilted.

Add the noodles, beansprouts and spring onions and stir-fry until heated through.

Vegetables and Noodles in Curry (Kari Sayur)

Serves 4

Ingredients

2 tsp peanut oil

½ tsp ground turmeric

1 tsp ground cumin

125 ml (4 fl oz) coconut milk

250 ml (8 fl oz) chicken stock

2 tsp brown sugar

1 head broccoli, cut into florets

½ cauliflower, cut into florets

1 carrot, sliced

1 lb 6 oz (600 g) fresh thin
   noodles

Paste

1 garlic clove, chopped

1 shallot, chopped

1 medium chilli, deseeded and
   chopped

2 tsp peanut oil

Method

Crush or pound the paste ingredients in a mortar with a pestle, or use a food processor.

Heat the remaining oil in a saucepan. Add the paste and stir-fry for 1–2 minutes. Add the turmeric and cumin and stir-fry until aromatic. Add the coconut milk, chicken stock, brown sugar, broccoli, cauliflower and carrot. Bring to the boil, then reduce the heat. Cover and cook for 6–8 minutes, or until the vegetables are tender. Stir in the noodles and serve.

Stuffed Fried Bean Curd Bags

Ingredients

10 pieces thin deep-fried tofu
  (aburage)
165 ml (5½ fl oz) dashi broth
3 tbsp/45 ml soy sauce
2 tbsp/25 ml sugar
1 tbsp/15 ml sake
375 ml (14 fl oz) sushi rice
1 tbsp/15 ml toasted sesame
  seeds
¼ grated boiled carrot

Method

Cut aburage into halves and pull open the center of the pieces, making bags. (Like preparing pita bread).

In a saucepan, combine dashi broth, soy sauce, sugar and sake. Bring to the boil and simmer the bean curd bags for 10–15 minutes. Remove from heat, drain and cool.

Mix the sushi rice with sesame seeds and carrot.

Fill the bags with the rice mixture and roll the top of the bean curd over the rice to enclose it. Be careful not to add too much rice or the bags will split.

Sour Vegetables (Sayur Asam)

Serves 4

Ingredients

1 tbsp peanut oil
1 tsp galangal powder
250 ml (8 fl oz) chicken stock
2 tbsp tamarind concentrate
1 tsp palm sugar or brown sugar
2 zucchinis (courgettes), sliced
1 eggplant (aubergine), diced, or
    3 baby eggplants (aubergines),
    sliced
115 g (4 oz) shredded cabbage
150 g (5 oz) green (French)
    beans

Paste

2 shallots, chopped
2 garlic cloves
2 medium chillies, deseeded and
    chopped
1 tsp shrimp paste (terasi)
Vegetable oil (optional)

Method

Crush or pound the paste ingredients in a mortar with a pestle or use a small food processor. If using a food processor you may need to add a little oil.

Heat the peanut oil in a wok or saucepan. Add the paste and galangal powder and cook for 1 minute. Add the chicken stock, tamarind and sugar. Bring to the boil, add the vegetables and cook for 6–8 minutes or until the vegetables are tender. Serve as a main or side dish.

Three Kinds of Deep-fried Tofu

Serves 4

Ingredients

1 block tofu, cut into 12 squares
arrowroot
3 tsp seaweed powder
3 tsp black sesame seeds
400 ml (14 fl oz) udonji
chives

Method

Lightly roll tofu cubes in arrowroot. Deep-fry tofu for 3–4 minutes.

Roll 4 cubes in seaweed powder to coat and roll 4 cubes in black sesame seeds.

Place one seaweed, one black sesame seed and one plain tofu cube in each serving bowl.

Pour 100 ml (3½ fl oz) of udonji into each bowl. Garnish with chives and serve.

Pak Choi In Oyster Sauce

Serves 4

Ingredients

400 g (14 oz) pak choi
3 tbsp oyster sauce
1 tbsp peanut oil
salt

Method

Trim the ends of pak choi stalks then separate the leaves and rinse thoroughly. Mix together oyster sauce and oil.

Put pak choi into a large saucepan of lightly salted boiling water and cook, uncovered, for 3 minutes or until tender. Drain thoroughly, return the pak choi to the pan, add oyster sauce and oil mixture and toss to coat evenly.

Salads

Thai Calamari Salad

Serves 4

Ingredients

12 calamari tubes, cleaned

200 g (7 oz) green beans, sliced
   lengthwise

2 medium sized tomatoes, cut
   into wedges

1 small green papaya, peeled,
   seeded and shredded

4 scallions/shallots, sliced

30 g (1 oz) fresh mint leaves

30 g (1 oz) fresh coriander
   (cilantro) leaves

1 fresh red chilli, chopped

Lime Dressing

2 tsp brown sugar

3 tbsp lime juice

1 tbsp fish sauce

pinch of salt

Method

Using a sharp knife, make a single cut down the length of each calamari tube and open it up. Cut parallel lines down the length of the calamari, taking care not to cut through the flesh. Make more cuts in the opposite direction to form a diamond pattern.

Heat a nonstick heavy-based skillet over a high heat, add calamari, and cook for 1–2 minutes each side or until tender. Remove from skillet and cut into thin strips.

Place calamari, beans, tomatoes, papaya, scallions, mint, coriander, and chilli in a serving bowl.

To make dressing, place sugar, lime juice, and fish sauce in a screw-top jar and shake well. Add salt to taste. Drizzle over salad and toss to combine. Cover and let stand for 20 minutes before serving.

Thai Beef Salad

Serves 4

Ingredients

500 g (1 lb 2 oz) round steak

salt and freshly ground black
   pepper

1 small red chilli, finely chopped

2 tbsp lime juice

2 tbsp fish sauce

2 tbsp brown sugar

1 tsp sesame oil

¼ Chinese cabbage, finely
   shredded

40 g (1½ oz) coriander
   (cilantro) sprigs

40 g (1½ oz) mint sprigs

125 g (4½ oz) snow peas,
   trimmed

1 cucumber, sliced

1 small red onion, thinly sliced

200 g (7 oz) cherry tomatoes,
   halved

Method

Trim any excess fat and sinew from the
steak. Season with salt and black pepper.

Cook the steak on a lightly oiled grill
pan for a few minutes until medium rare.
Remove and rest for 10 minutes before
slicing across the grain into thin strips.

Put the chilli, lime juice, fish sauce, brown
sugar, and sesame oil in a small bowl and
whisk to combine.

Combine the cabbage, half the coriander,
the mint, snow peas, cucumber, onion,
and tomatoes on a large salad platter or a
individual plates.

Top with the sliced steak, drizzle with
dressing, and garnish with the remaining
coriander.

Asian Gingered Coleslaw

Serves 6

Ingredients

½ Napa cabbage, very finely sliced

4 baby bok choy, leaves separated and sliced

8 spring onions (scallions), julienned

200 g (7 oz) canned sliced water chestnuts, drained

2 medium carrots, finely julienned

2 stalks lemongrass, finely sliced

4 kaffir lime leaves, finely sliced

Garnish

1 bunch coriander (cilantro), roughly chopped

75 g (3 oz) toasted peanuts or sunflower seeds

Dressing

2 tbsp mayonnaise

2 tbsp plain yogurt

juice of 2 lemons

juice of 1 lime

5 cm (2 in) piece ginger, grated

60 ml (2 fl oz) rice vinegar

salt and freshly ground black pepper

Method

Finely slice the cabbage and mix in a large bowl with the sliced bok choy, scallions, water chestnuts, carrots, and finely sliced lemongrass and lime leaves. Toss thoroughly.

In a small bowl, whisk together all the dressing ingredients until smooth and well seasoned, then pour it over the salad ingredients and toss thoroughly until all the vegetables are coated with the dressing.

Just before serving, add the coriander and sprinkle with the peanuts or sunflower seeds.

Chicken Salad

Serves 6-8

Ingredients

1 kg (2 lb) lean chicken, diced

1 tsp salt

1 tsp pepper

1 tsp paprika

1 tsp ground cumin

1 tsp onion powder

475 ml (16 fl oz) orange juice

60 ml (2 fl oz) dry white wine

2 onions, diced

60 g (2½ oz) apricot jelly

60 g (2½ oz) peach jelly

85 g (3 oz) honey

2 tbsp lemon juice

2 tbsp lime juice

500 g (1 lb 2 oz) fresh or
 canned kumquats

40 g (1½ oz) wild rice

50 g (2 oz) brown rice

250 ml (8 fl oz) white rice

1 bunch basil, leaves thinly sliced

125 g (4½ oz) toasted pistachio
 nuts, chopped

Method

Place the diced chicken in a plastic bag and add the salt, pepper, paprika, ground cumin, and onion powder and seal the bag. Shake vigorously to coat the chicken with the spice mix, then thread the spiced chicken pieces onto wooden skewers and place them in a shallow baking dish. Set aside.

Meanwhile mix the orange juice, wine, onions, both jellies, honey, lemon juice, lime juice, and kumquats in a saucepan and heat until just about to boil. Season to taste. Pour half this mixture (reserving the remaining mixture) over the chicken skewers and marinate for 2 hours.

While the chicken is marinating, prepare the rice. Bring a large pot of salted water to a boil and add the wild rice. Boil for 5 minutes then add the brown rice. Boil these together for a further 10 minutes before adding the white rice and simmering for 15 minutes. Drain thoroughly and keep warm.

Heat a grill pan, barbecue, or broiler and cook the chicken skewers until cooked through, brushing them with the remaining kumquat mixture as they cook.

Fold the finely sliced fresh basil and chopped pistachio nuts through the rice then serve with the chicken skewers. Drizzle with any remaining kumquat mixture with if desired.

Duck Salad

Serves 4

Ingredients

2 tbsp vinegar

2½ tbsp sugar

2 tbsp peanut oil

2 tbsp soy sauce

1 tsp mustard, home-mixed or
    prepared

pinch of salt

125 g (4½ oz) carrot

125 g (4½ oz) cucumber

100 g (3½ oz) bok choy or
    cabbage

500 g (1 lb 2 oz) cooked duck
    meat

Method

Mix dressing of vinegar, sugar, peanut oil, soy sauce, mustard and salt thoroughly. Shred carrot and cucumber into paper thin strips with a potato peeler. Cut end off bok choy, wash leaves very carefully and shred as thinly as possible.

Arrange vegetables on a serving plate and top with shredded duck. Add dressing just before serving.

Note: Salads are rarely prepared in China, except at luxury hotels. However this recipe will use up leftover whole duck from other dishes. Substitute chicken if desired.

Shelley's Cabbage and Chinese Noodle Salad

Serves 4

Ingredients

Salad

½ curly green cabbage

4 baby bok choy

8 spring onions, (scallions)

½ bunch fresh coriander
  (cilantro)

125 g (4½ oz) flaked almonds

60 g (2½ oz) pine nuts

100 g (3½ oz) cooked Chinese
  noodles

Dressing

4 tbsp peanut oil

2 tbsp balsamic vinegar

2 tbsp fresh lime or lemon juice

1 tbsp brown sugar (optional)

1 tbsp soy sauce

salt and cracked pepper to taste

Method

Finely shred cabbage and transfer to a large mixing bowl. Thoroughly wash bok choy then slice widthways and add to cabbage.

Wash spring onions then slice finely on the diagonal. Add to cabbage mixture together with the washed and roughly chopped coriander.

Under the griller or in a dry fry pan, toast almonds and pine nuts and set aside to cool. Alternatively, toast nuts in a microwave by spreading nuts over the microwave plate and cooking them on high for 2 minutes. Mix gently to distribute then cook for a few more minutes until the nuts are as golden as you wish. Allow to cool.

Mix the nuts and noodles with cabbage salad. To make the dressing, beat all the ingredients together with a whisk until thick. Drizzle over the salad, toss thoroughly then serve immediately.

Desserts

Citrus Fruit Salad With Ginger

Serves 4

Ingredients

1 pink grapefruit

1 large orange

1 tangerine, peeled and divided
into segments

rind of 1 lime, pared with a
vegetable peeler and cut into
matchsticks

55 g (2 oz) cumquats, halved
and pips removed

juice of 1 small lemon

150 ml (5 fl oz) ginger beer

3 tbsp caster sugar

2 pieces stem ginger in
syrup, drained and finely
chopped

fresh mint to decorate

Method

Slice tops and bottoms off grapefruit
and orange, using a sharp, serrated knife.
Cut down the side of the fruits, following
the curves, to remove the skin and pith.
Hold fruit over a bowl to catch the juices
and cut out the segments, leaving the
membranes behind. Place in a serving
dish with tangerine segments. Reserve the
fruit juices.

Place lime rind and cumquats in a
saucepan with water. Simmer for 10
minutes or until softened. Add cumquats
to the other fruit and drain lime rind on
kitchen towels. Reserve the liquid.

Add lemon juice, ginger beer, sugar and
any juices from the fruit to the reserved
cooking liquid. Heat gently, stirring, for
5 minutes or until sugar dissolves. Pour
mixture over fruit and stir in chopped
ginger. Sprinkle with lime rind and
fresh mint.

Oriental Fruit Salad

Serves 4

Ingredients

3 stalks lemongrass

55 g (2 oz) caster sugar

100 ml (3½ fl oz) water

1 small rock melon

1 mango

400 g (14 oz) can lychees,
    drained

fresh mint leaves to garnish

Method

Peel outer layers from lemongrass stalks, finely chop lower white bulbous parts and discard fibrous tops. Place lemongrass, sugar and water in a saucepan. Simmer, stirring, for 5 minutes or until the sugar dissolves, then bring to the boil. Remove from the heat and leave to cool for 20 minutes. Refrigerate for 30 minutes.

Halve melon and scrape out seeds. Cut into wedges, then remove skin and cut flesh into small chunks. Slice off the 2 fat sides of the mango close to the stone. Cut a criss-cross pattern across the flesh (but not through the skin) of each piece, then push the skin inside out to expose the cubes of flesh and cut them off.

Place melon, mango and lychees in serving bowls. Strain lemongrass syrup and pour over the fruit. Decorate with mint.

Coconut Pancakes (Dadar Gulang)

Makes 8

Ingredients

55 g (2 oz) plain (all-purpose)
    flour
1 tbsp caster (superfine) sugar
2 eggs, lightly beaten
175 ml (6 fl oz) milk or
    coconut milk
Oil spray, for cooking
175 g (6 oz) grated palm sugar
    or brown sugar
125 ml (4 fl oz) water
1 pandan leaf
115 g (4 oz) shredded coconut,
    toasted
1 papaya, diced
Ice cream, to serve

Method

Combine the flour and sugar in a mixing
bowl. Add the eggs and milk and whisk
until the mixture is smooth. Add a little
water if it is too thick.

Heat a frying pan. Spray with oil, then add
enough mixture to make a thin pancake.
Cook the pancakes for 1–2 minutes on
each side.

Combine the palm sugar, water and
pandan leaf in a saucepan. Bring to the
boil and simmer over low heat, stirring
until the sugar dissolves and the syrup
thickens slightly.

Place the coconut and papaya on each
pancake and roll up. Serve the pancakes
with ice cream and drizzle with syrup.

Fried Banana Cakes (Pisang Goreng)

Serves 4

Ingredients

6 medium ripe bananas, peeled
1 tbsp white (granulated) sugar
1 tbsp plain (all-purpose) flour
Oil, for deep-frying

Method

Mash the bananas and mix with the sugar and sifted flour. Heat the oil in a wok and drop in a large spoonful of batter. Cook several at a time, but do not overcrowd the wok or the temperature of the oil will be lowered. When the cakes are crisp and golden brown, drain on kitchen paper. Serve warm.

Black Rice Pudding (Bubur Injin)

Serves 4–6

Ingredients

300 g (10½ oz) black glutinous rice

1 litre (1¾ pints) water

1 pandan leaf

75 g (3 oz) palm sugar syrup (see below)

Coconut milk or ice cream to serve

Palm Sugar Syrup

150 g (5 oz) grated palm sugar or brown sugar

125 ml (4 fl oz) water

Method

Rinse the rice under cold running water for 1–2 minutes, or until the water is clear.

Combine the rice, water and pandan leaf in a large saucepan. Bring to the boil and simmer over low heat for 40 minutes. Add the syrup and cook for another 10 minutes, or until the rice is tender and the liquid has been absorbed.

To make the syrup, combine the sugar and water in a small saucepan. Bring to the boil and simmer for 8–10 minutes.

Serve with coconut milk or ice cream.

Rum And Lime Banana Fritters

Serves 4

Ingredients

4 bananas
juice of 1 lime
2 tsp caster sugar
1 tbsp dark rum
oil for deep-frying

Batter

100 g (3½ oz) self-raising flour
pinch of salt
150 ml (5 fl oz) water
2 tbsp sesame seeds

Method

Peel each banana and cut in half crossways, then slice lengthways to make quarters. Place banana quarters, lime juice, sugar and rum in a deep, non-metallic dish and mix gently. Cover and set aside for 30 minutes to marinate.

Meanwhile, make the batter. Sift flour and salt into a mixing bowl. Pour in 150 ml (5 fl oz) of water and whisk to form a smooth, thick batter. Stir in sesame seeds and set aside.

Heat 5 cm (2 in) of oil in a wok or a large, deep frying-pan until smoking hot. Coat banana pieces thoroughly in batter. Fry for 5 minutes or until golden brown, then turn over and cook for 2 minutes to brown the other side (you may have to cook them in batches). Drain on kitchen towels.

Toffee Apples

Serves 4

Ingredients

4 medium cooking apples
plain flour for dusting
1.5 litres (2½ pints) plus 1 tbsp
   of sesame oil
125 g (4½ oz) sugar
3 tsp sesame seeds
iced water for serving

Batter

2 eggs, beaten
75 g (3 oz) cornflour
50 g (2 oz) flour
a little water

Method

To make batter, add beaten eggs to flours. Pour in enough water to make a reasonably thick batter.

Peel, core and cut apples into 2½ cm wedges, dip in dusting flour and dunk into batter before deep-frying at moderate heat in 1.5 litres (2½ pints) of oil. Use extra tablespoon of oil to coat a large serving plate.

When carefully turned apple wedges have softened and turned golden (after a minute or so), drain them and place aside. Heat sugar carefully until melted and golden and toffee-coloured. Quickly add apple wedges and cook for 1 minute. Add sesame seeds and toss apple pieces until all are coated. Dip apple pieces into iced water.

Serve on the oiled plate immediately.

Note: The iced water, if the apples are dipped into it quickly, will solidify the toffee instantly. Use this same method to present potato, yam, water chestnuts, banana, pineapple and even frozen custard or ice-cream balls in a similar manner. Be careful not to splatter the hot toffee.

Mandarins In Almond Lake

Serves 4

Ingredients

590 ml (1 pint) milk

100 g (3½ oz) sugar

1 tsp almond essence

75 g (3 oz) ground rice

315 g (11 oz) can mandarin
   segments, canned

40 g (1½ oz) flaked almonds

Method

In a saucepan, combine milk, sugar, almond essence and rice. Stir continuously and bring to the boil. Simmer, still stirring, for 5 minutes. Transfer to a bowl, cover and cool completely.

Drain mandarins. Spoon rice into individual dishes. Arrange mandarins on top and sprinkle with almond flakes.

Sushi and Sashimi Techniques

Preparing Sushi Rice (Shari or Sushi Meshi)

Ingredients

1 litre (35 fl oz) short grain rice
1 litre (35 fl oz) water

Sushi vinegar:

125 ml (4 fl oz) rice vinegar
60 ml (2 fl oz) 4 tbsp sugar
2 tsp/10 ml salt
1 tsp/5 ml soy sauce

Method

Rice cooked for sushi should be slightly harder in texture than for other dishes. You will need approximately 250 ml (8 fl oz) of cooked rice for each roll. It is easier and better to make too much rice than too little. Every recipe for sushi rice is different, but they all work. You might find a recipe on the bottle of rice vinegar, on the bag of rice, or on the package of nori.

Most recipes call for rinsing the raw rice until the water runs clear, but it can be avoided. The reason it is rinsed first is to remove talc from the rice. Most rice seems to be coated now with some sort of cereal starch, rather than talc, so rinsing could be omitted. Tradition also suggests letting the rinsed rice drain in a colander, or zaru, for 30–60 minutes. It's up to you. The rice you use should be short-grained rice.

Wash rice until water is clear (optional).

Combine the rice and water in a sauce pan and set aside for 30 minutes.

Bring rice and water to boil.

Reduce heat to very low and simmer for 10 minutes.

Turn off heat and leave for 20 minutes to steam.

Combine ingredients for sushi vineagar in a pan and heat, stirring, until dissolved.

Place the hot rice in a bowl and then sprinkle the sushi vinegar over the rice and mix it as if cutting. Use a fan to cool until it reaches room temperature.

Preparing Sushi Rice
(Shari or Sushi Meshi)

1 Rinse a Japanese wooden bowl (hangiri) or a flat wooden or plastic bowl with cold water before you place in the hot rice.

2 Add the sushi vinegar to the rice, pouring it over a paddle to help evenly dispense the vinegar.

3 Mix the vinegar into the rice, being careful not the flatten the rice.

4 Use a fan to help bring the rice back to room temperature.

Making Nigiri-Sushi

Method

Most important when making nigiri-sushi is the balance between the topping and the rice. It is hand-formed by gently squeezing the ingredients together. You need a chopping-board, a sharp knife and a bowl of vinegared water (tezu) in which to rinse the fingers, the fish and the prepared rice. Remember, one of the most important criteria of well-made sushi is that the rice does not break when you pick it up.

1 Prepare the tezu, which consists of half water, half sushi vinegar. Moisten fingers and palms with the tezu. Most beginners put too much water on their hands. Use only a small amount.

2 Pick up a piece of fish in one hand, and with the other a small handfull of prepared sushi rice. Gently squeeze the rice to form a block. Most beginners hold too much rice. Take less than you think you need.

With the piece of fish laying in the lm of your hand, a small amount of sabi can be spread along the fish.

4 With the piece of fish still in your palm, the rice can be placed on top of the fish. Use your thumb and press down slightly on the rice, making a small depression.

5 Using the forefinger from the other hand, press down on the rice, causing it to flatten.

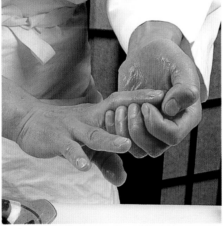

Turn the sushi over (fish side up) d, using the thumb and middle ger, squeeze the rice together.

7 Position fingers and hand as above, covering the fish and rice. Gently squeeze around the sushi. Repeat steps 5–7 twice more.

8 You should now have a piece of finished sushi, with the fish covering the firm rice.

Making Thin Sushi Rolls (Hosomaki)

1 Cut one nori sheet in half lengthwise and trim the sides so they're straight. Use two pieces for making the sushi rolls. Place nori shiny side down onto the mat.

2 Moisten your hands with some tezu and get a handful of rice from the rice-cooling tub. Spread the rice over the nori, taking care to do this evenly.

3 With your forefinger, spread the desired amount of wasabi across the rice, starting at one end and spreading it across the middle to the other end.

4 Place filling along the center of the rice, on top of the wasabi. Lift the edge of the bamboo mat.

5 With fingers from both hands hold onto the mat and the filling. Wrap the mat and nori over the filling, making sure all ingredients are evenly pressed.

6 Continue rolling, but applying a little more pressure to compact the rice. If needed, repeat the last step again to ensure the rice is pressed firmly and evenly along the roll.

7 Remove roll from the mat and place on a cutting board. Cut the roll in half.

8 Generally allow 6 pieces per roll, so lay the 2 halves next to each other and cut into thirds.

Making Temaki-Sushi

1 Start by picking up a half sheet of nori in one hand and a handful of rice about the size of a golf ball in the other.

2 Place rice on one side of the nori sheet and start spreading it out, covering only half of the nori sheet.

3 With your finger or a spoon, rub the desired amount of wasabi along the rice.

4 Add desired fillings to the roll, placing them from one corner down to the middle of the opposite side.

5 Fold the nearest corner of the nori over the filling, and start to shape into a cone.

6 The finished temaki-sushi should coned-shaped with no rice falling o from the bottom.

Making Thick Sushi Rolls (Futomaki)

1 Cut one nori sheet in half lengthwise and straighten the sides. Lay ½ sheet of nori shiny side down onto the bamboo rolling mat.

2 Moisten your hands with some tezu and get a handful of sushi rice. Spread the rice evenly over the surface of the nori.

3 Add the desired amount of wasabi along the middle of the rice.

4 And also some Japanese mayonnaise.

5 Add the fillings you wish to use, placing them in the middle and on top of the wasabi and mayonnaise.

6 Start rolling the mat up over the ingredients, stopping when you get to about 1in/2¹/₂cm away from the end of the nori.

7 Lift the mat up and roll forward again to join the edges of the nori together, while at the same time applying a small amount of pressure to make the roll firm.

8 Using a sharp knife, cut the completed rolls in half, place the halves next to each other and cut into thirds. Each roll will provide 6 pieces.

Index

US: $19.99
UK: £16.99